YUMMY SOUP AND Salad RECIPES

Jennifer S. Larson   Photographs by **Brie Cohen**

M MILLBROOK PRESS • MINNEAPOLIS

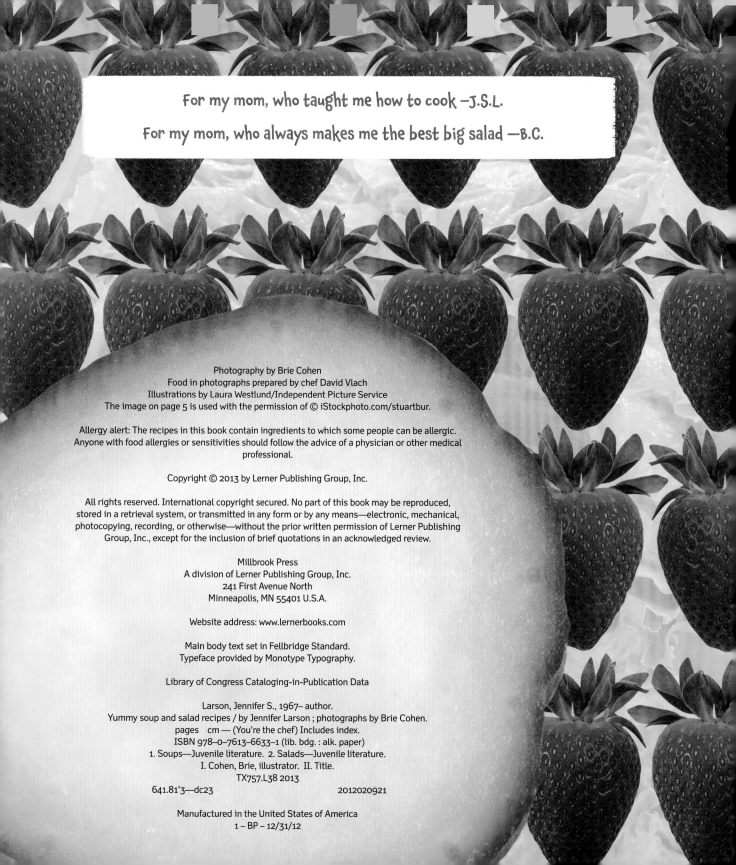

For my mom, who taught me how to cook —J.S.L.

For my mom, who always makes me the best big salad —B.C.

Photography by Brie Cohen
Food in photographs prepared by chef David Vlach
Illustrations by Laura Westlund/Independent Picture Service
The image on page 5 is used with the permission of © iStockphoto.com/stuartbur.

Allergy alert: The recipes in this book contain ingredients to which some people can be allergic. Anyone with food allergies or sensitivities should follow the advice of a physician or other medical professional.

Millbrook Press
A division of Lerner Publishing Group, Inc.
241 First Avenue North
Minneapolis, MN 55401 U.S.A.

Website address: www.lernerbooks.com

Main body text set in Fellbridge Standard.
Typeface provided by Monotype Typography.

Library of Congress Cataloging-in-Publication Data

Larson, Jennifer S., 1967– author.
Yummy soup and salad recipes / by Jennifer Larson ; photographs by Brie Cohen.
pages   cm — (You're the chef) Includes index.
ISBN 978–0–7613–6633–1 (lib. bdg. : alk. paper)
1. Soups—Juvenile literature. 2. Salads—Juvenile literature.
I. Cohen, Brie, illustrator. II. Title.
TX757.L38 2013
641.81'3—dc23   2012020921

Manufactured in the United States of America
1 – BP – 12/31/12

TABLE of CONTENTS

Are you ready to make some tasty soups and salads? YOU can be the chef and make food for yourself and your family. These easy recipes are perfect for a chef who is just learning to cook. And they're so delicious, you'll want to make them again and again!

I developed these recipes with the help of my kids, who are seven and ten years old. They can't do all the cooking on their own yet, but they can do a lot.

Can't get enough of cooking? Check out www.lerneresource.com for bonus recipes, healthful eating tips, links to cooking technique videos, metric conversions, and more!

BEFORE YOU START

Reserve your space! Always ask for permission to work in the kitchen.

Find a helper! You will need an adult helper for some tasks. Talk with this person to decide what steps you can do on your own and what steps the adult will help with.

Make a plan! Read through the whole recipe before you start cooking. Do you have the ingredients you'll need? If you don't know what a certain ingredient is, see page 31 to find out more. Do you understand each step? If you don't understand a technique, such as *simmer* or *slice*, turn to page 7. At the beginning of each recipe, you'll see how much time you'll need to prepare the recipe and to cook it. The recipe will also tell you how many servings it makes. Small drawings at the top of each recipe let you know what major kitchen equipment you'll need—such as a stovetop, a blender, or a microwave.

stovetop

blender

knives

microwave

oven

Wash up! Always wash your hands with soap and water before you start cooking. And wash them again after you touch raw eggs, meat, or fish.

Get it together! Find the tools you'll use, such as measuring cups or a mixing bowl. Gather all the ingredients you'll need. That way you won't have to stop to look for things once you start cooking.

SAFETY TIPS

That's sharp! Your adult helper needs to be in the kitchen when you are using a knife, a grater, or a peeler. If you are doing the cutting, use a cutting board. Cut away from your body, and keep your fingers away from the blade.

That's hot! Be sure an adult is in the kitchen if you use the stove or the oven. Your adult helper can help you cook on the stove and take hot things out of the oven.

Tie it back! If you have long hair, tie it back or wear a hat. If you have long sleeves, roll them up. You want to keep your hair and clothing out of the food and away from flames or other heat sources.

Turn that handle! When cooking on the stove, turn the pot handle toward the back. That way, no one will accidentally bump the pot and knock it off the stove.

Wash it! If you are working with raw eggs or meat, you need to keep things extra clean. After cutting raw meat or fish, wash the knife and the cutting board right away. They must be clean before you use them to cut anything else.

Go slowly! Take your time when you're working. When you are doing something for the first time, such as peeling or grating, be sure not to rush.

Above all, have fun!

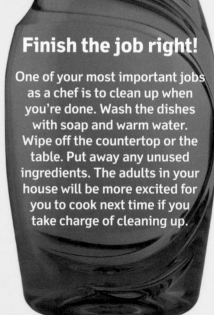

Finish the job right!

One of your most important jobs as a chef is to clean up when you're done. Wash the dishes with soap and warm water. Wipe off the countertop or the table. Put away any unused ingredients. The adults in your house will be more excited for you to cook next time if you take charge of cleaning up.

COOKING TOOLS

baking sheets

blender

bowls

can opener

colander

cooling rack

cutting board

dish towel

dry measuring cups

fork

frying pan

grater

knives

ladle

large pot

large spoon

liquid measuring cup

measuring spoons

oven mitt

pizza cutter

saucepans

serrated knife

vegetable peeler

whisk

wooden spoon

TECHNIQUES

bake: to cook in the oven

boil: to heat liquid on a stovetop until the liquid starts to bubble

chop: to cut food into small pieces using a knife

cover: to put a lid on a pan or pot containing food

discard: to throw away or put in a compost bin. Discarded parts of fruits and vegetables and eggshells can be put in a compost bin, if you have one.

drain: to pour the liquid off a food. You can drain food by pouring it into a colander or strainer. If you are draining water or juice from canned food, you can also use the lid to hold the food back while the liquid pours out.

grate: to use a food grater to shred food into small pieces

mix: to stir food using a spoon or fork

preheat: to turn the oven to the temperature you will need for baking. An oven takes about 15 minutes to heat up.

puree: to blend until smooth

serrated: a tool, such as a knife, that has a bumpy edge

set aside: to put nearby in a bowl or plate or on a clean work space

shred: to cut or grate into small pieces

simmer: to boil at a low heat setting. The liquid will be boiling with very tiny bubbles.

slice: to cut food into thin pieces

sprinkle: to scatter on top

MEASURING

To measure **dry ingredients**, such as sugar or flour, spoon the ingredient into a measuring cup until it is full. Then use the back of a butter knife to level it off. Do not pack it down unless the recipe tells you to. Do not use measuring cups made for liquids.

When you're measuring a **liquid**, such as milk or water, use a clear glass or plastic measuring cup. Set the cup on the table or a counter and pour the liquid into the cup. Pour slowly and stop when the liquid has reached the correct line.

Don't measure your ingredients over the bowl they will go into. If you accidentally spill, you might have way too much!

serves 4

preparation time: 30 to 45 minutes
cooking time: 15 minutes

ingredients:

½ cup fresh spinach
2 green onions
1 egg
1 tablespoon soy sauce
½ pound ground chicken
¼ teaspoon salt
pepper
20 wonton wrappers (or 5 egg roll
   skins cut into four equal pieces)
8 cups water
3 cup chicken broth
¼ cup frozen peas

equipment:

knife
cutting board
measuring cups—¼ cup, ½ cup
medium bowl
fork
measuring spoons
small bowl
large pot
liquid measuring cup
wooden spoon
colander
medium saucepan
4 bowls for serving

Chicken Wonton Soup

Have fun making dumplings for this tasty, Chinese soup.

1. **Wash** the spinach under cool water. Use the knife and cutting board to remove the spinach stems. Make a stack of spinach leaves and **cut** into large pieces.

2. **Wash** the green onions. Next, **cut** off the roots. Remove any dry or wilted green parts. Then **slice** the onions into small pieces about ½ inch long. You can use both the white and green parts of the onion. Set aside the spinach and onions.

3. In a medium bowl, crack egg and **beat** with a fork. **Add** soy sauce, ground chicken, salt, and a few shakes of pepper. **Mix** well with fork. This is the filling. It will go inside the wontons.

4. **Fill** a small bowl halfway with water. Put it on a clean work space where you will fold your wontons.

5. Set a wonton wrapper on your work space. **Spoon** 1 teaspoon of filling in the center of the wonton.

6. **Dip** your finger in the water, and run your finger along two sides of the wonton wrapper (see diagram). After the edge is wet, **fold** the wonton in half diagonally so that the dry sides match up with the wet sides. **Press** along the edges with your fingers to seal the wonton. Repeat steps 4 and 5 for the remaining 19 wontons.

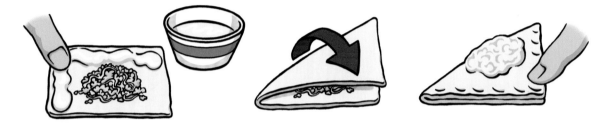

Turn the page for more Chicken Wonton Soup

Chicken Wonton Soup continued

7. In a large pot, bring 8 cups water to a boil. Use a wooden spoon to **drop** the wontons, one at a time, into boiling water. Simmer uncovered 7 to 8 minutes until wontons float to the top.

8. Set a colander in the sink. Get some help to gently **pour** the wontons and water into the colander to drain. **Rinse** wontons with cold water.

9. In a medium saucepan, bring the chicken broth to a boil. Then **add** peas, green onions, and spinach. **Stir** until the spinach is wilted, about 2 to 3 minutes. Turn off heat.

10. **Spoon** some soup into each bowl. **Add** 5 wontons to each bowl. Enjoy!

TRY THIS!

Replace the ground chicken with ½ pound **ground pork** or **ground beef**.

Replace the spinach with **bok choy**. Wash the bok choy under cool water. Cut off the thick stem at the bottom. Separate a few leaves. Cut the leaves into large pieces. Add the bok choy to the soup when you would add the spinach. Cook for 3 to 5 minutes.

Chillin' Chili

A hot bowl of chili is tasty on a chilly day—or anytime. Serve it with some bread or crackers.

1. Use the can opener to **open** the tomatoes and beans. Set aside the can of tomatoes. Put a colander in the sink, and **pour** the beans into the colander to drain the liquid.

2. **Wash** the green pepper and carrots in cool water.

Turn the page for more Chillin' Chili

serves 4 to 6

preparation time: 20 minutes
cooking time: 25 minutes

ingredients:

1 28-ounce can chopped tomatoes
1 14-ounce can black beans
1 14-ounce can pinto beans
1 green pepper
2 carrots
1 medium onion
2 tablespoons vegetable oil
2 teaspoon chili powder
1 teaspoon garlic powder
1 teaspoon cumin
1½ cups vegetable stock or water
4 ounces (1 cup) cheddar cheese
1 cup frozen corn
½ teaspoon salt
pepper

equipment:

can opener
colander
knife
cutting board
grater
large pot
wooden spoon
measuring spoons
liquid measuring cup
measuring cup—1 cup
ladle
4 to 6 bowls for serving

3. Use the knife and cutting board to cut the vegetables. **Cut** around the stem of the green pepper. Then cut the green pepper in half and remove the seeds. Discard the stem and seeds. **Chop** the rest of the green pepper. Set aside.

4. **Cut** off both ends of the onion. Set the onion on one of the flat parts you made by cutting it. Cut the onion in half. **Peel** off and discard the papery layers around the outside. Lay the onion half flat on the cutting board. **Cut** the onion crosswise into semicircular slices. Then **chop** the slices into small pieces. Repeat with the other half. Set aside.

5. **Grate** the carrots using the grater. Discard the stem. Set aside grated carrot.

6. **Pour** the vegetable oil into a large cooking pot. Turn on the burner under the pot to high. **Add** the onions and cook 5 minutes. **Stir** them with the wooden spoon a few times every minute.

7. **Add** the green pepper, chili powder, garlic powder, and cumin. **Stir** and cook 5 more minutes.

8. **Stir** in the carrots, tomatoes with their juice, the drained beans, and stock or water. **Cover** the pot until the chili comes to a boil. Turn the heat down to low and cook 15 minutes.

9. While the chili is cooking, rinse and dry the grater. Then **grate** 1 cup of cheddar cheese. Set aside.

10. **Add** corn, salt, and a sprinkle of pepper to the cooking pot. Turn off heat.

11. **Ladle** the chili into bowls. Serve with grated cheese on top.

TRY THIS!

You can add meat to your chili if you like. Add 1 pound **ground beef** to the pan after you cook the onions in step 6. Cook until the meat has turned color from pink to brown. Have an adult drain the grease from the pan. Then continue with step 7. Serve with **sour cream** on top instead of cheese.

For a **thicker chili**, you can add **pasta**. Use a smaller shape such as macaroni. Look at the pasta package for cooking time. If the pasta takes 8 minutes to cook, stir in ½ cup pasta 8 minutes before you're ready to serve the chili. (You might also need to add a little extra water if the chili gets too thick.)

serves 4

preparation time: 25 minutes
cooking time: 20 to 25 minutes

ingredients:

1 stalk celery
1 carrot
2 large red potatoes
1 small onion
2 tablespoons vegetable oil
1 cup water
1 14-ounce can creamed corn
1 cup milk
¼ teaspoon salt
pepper

equipment:

knife
cutting board
grater
measuring spoons
medium saucepan
wooden spoon
can opener
liquid measuring cup
fork

Hearty Corn Chowder

This corn chowder will fill you up. Chowder is a thick soup or stew, often made with milk or cream.

1. **Wash** the celery, carrot, and potatoes under cool water.

2. Use the knife and cutting board to cut vegetables. **Cut** off both ends of the onion. Set the onion on one of the flat parts you made by cutting it. Cut the onion in half. **Peel** off and discard the papery layers around the outside. Lay the onion half flat on the cutting board. **Cut** the onion crosswise into semicircular slices. Then **chop** the slices into small pieces. Repeat with the other half. Set aside.

3. **Cut** the bottom edge off the celery. **Slice** the rest of the celery into semicircles. Set aside with the onion.

4. **Cut** the potatoes into small pieces, about ½-inch size. **Grate** the carrot with a grater. Set both aside.

5. **Pour** the vegetable oil into a medium saucepan. Turn on the burner under the pan to high. Cook the onion and celery in the oil for 5 minutes, **stirring** often.

6. **Add** the water, potatoes, and carrot. Bring to a boil. Turn down to low heat, and simmer until potatoes and carrots are cooked (about 10 minutes). They are cooked when you can easily pierce them with a fork.

7. Use the can opener to **open** the corn. **Add** corn and milk to the saucepan and simmer for 5 more minutes. **Add** the salt and a sprinkle of pepper. Serve.

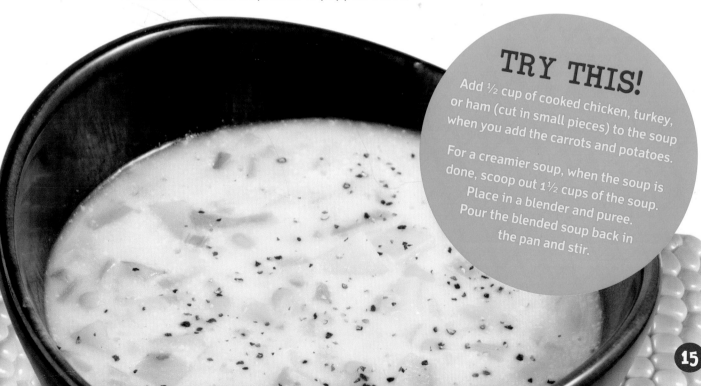

TRY THIS!

Add ½ cup of cooked chicken, turkey, or ham (cut in small pieces) to the soup when you add the carrots and potatoes.

For a creamier soup, when the soup is done, scoop out 1½ cups of the soup. Place in a blender and puree. Pour the blended soup back in the pan and stir.

serves 4

preparation time: 30 minutes
cooking time: 0 minutes

ingredients:
2 medium cucumbers
1½ cups plain yogurt
2 tablespoons honey
2 tablespoons fresh mint

equipment:
vegetable peeler
knife
cutting board
measuring cups—1 cup, ½ cup
measuring spoons
blender (or food processor)
wooden spoon or rubber spatula
4 bowls for serving

Cool as a Cucumber Soup

This refreshing soup will make you cool as a cucumber.
Serve it with bread, cheese slices, and a fruit salad
(see page 24) for a cool summer meal.

1. **Wash** the cucumbers in cool water. Use a vegetable peeler to **peel** cucumbers. (If you are using smaller cucumbers fresh from the garden or farmer's market, you don't need to peel them.) Use the knife and cutting board to cut off the ends of the cucumbers. **Slice** the cucumbers. Then chop them into ½ inch pieces.

2. Place yogurt and half of the cucumbers in the blender (or food processor). **Blend** until smooth.

3. **Add** the remaining cucumbers and honey. **Blend** again until smooth. If you have trouble getting the mixture to blend, add a small amount of water. Use a wooden spoon or rubber spatula if you need to mix. NEVER put your hand into a food processor or blender. **Pour** soup into bowls.

4. **Wash** the mint in cool water. **Tear** the leaves into small pieces or cut with a knife. **Sprinkle** a little mint on top of each bowl of soup.

A note about mint:

You can find mint at a grocery store with other herbs. Many people also grow it in their gardens. Maybe you have a neighbor who will share a few mint leaves with you. If you don't have space for a garden, mint and other herbs can be fun to grow in a pot outside or in a sunny window. Then you can use them in your food creations any time you want.

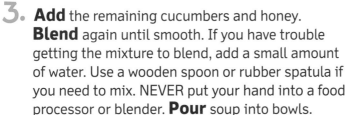

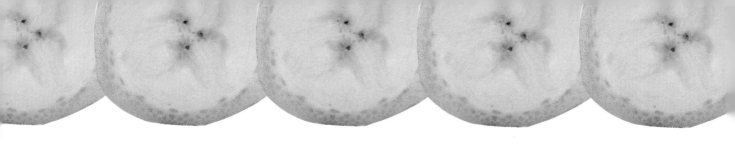

Fruity Dessert Soup

Who said soup is just for lunch or dinner? Try this fruity soup for dessert or for an afternoon snack.

serves 2

preparation time: 20 minutes
cooking time: 0 minutes

ingredients:

1 cup fresh or frozen strawberries
1 banana
1 teaspoon fresh mint or 2
    tablespoons chocolate chips
1 cup vanilla yogurt
½ cup orange juice

equipment:

colander
knife
cutting board
measuring cup—1 cup
measuring spoons
liquid measuring cup
blender
2 bowls for serving

1. If you are using fresh strawberries, **wash** them under cool water. Use the knife and cutting board to **cut** off the green tops. If you are using frozen strawberries, measure them.

2. **Peel** the banana.

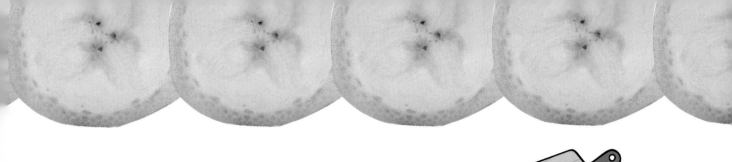

3. If using the mint, **wash** it in cool water. **Tear** into small pieces, or **cut** with a knife. Set aside.

4. Put fruit, yogurt, and orange juice in the blender. **Puree**. Pour the soup into two bowls. **Sprinkle** each bowl with fresh mint or chocolate chips.

TRY THIS!

The sky's the limit! Try some other fresh or frozen fruit: kiwi, blueberries, or pineapple. Sprinkle some shredded coconut or nuts on top.

serves 4

preparation time: 30 to 45 minutes
cooking time: 10 minutes

ingredients:
4 to 8 large whole lettuce leaves
toppings:
1 egg
3 cups water
1 small tomato
1 cucumber
1 green pepper
½ apple
½ avocado
1 carrot
2 ounces (½ cup) cheddar cheese
¼ cup sliced black olives
   (you can buy them already sliced)
¼ cup raisins or dried cranberries
¼ cup sunflower seeds
dressing:
¼ cup mayonnaise
1 tablespoon white vinegar
2 tablespoons apple juice

equipment:
small saucepan
large spoon
12 small bowls or containers
serrated knife
cutting board
vegetable peeler
grater
measuring cups—¼ cup
measuring spoons
medium bowl
fork or whisk
dish towel
4 plates for serving

Salad Rollups

Diners can all choose their own
ingredients in this rolled-up salad.

1. **Place** water and egg in a small saucepan. Turn on high heat. When the water starts to boil, turn down to low. Boil for 10 minutes. Carefully **remove** egg from water with a large spoon. Run egg under cold water. When egg is cool, tap it gently on a hard surface to break the shell. **Peel** off the shell. **Cut** egg into small pieces. Put in a small bowl.

2. **Wash** the tomato, cucumber, green pepper, carrot, and apple under cool water. Use the knife and cutting board to cut each. It works best to cut a tomato with a serrated knife, which is a knife with bumps along the sharp edge. To cut the tomato, first cut out the green or brown circle on the top. Discard it. Then **chop** the rest of the tomato. Put in a small bowl.

3. To cut the cucumber, first **peel** with a vegetable peeler. Cut off and discard ends. **Cut** in slices. Then **chop** into smaller pieces. Put in a small bowl.

4. To cut the green pepper, first **cut** around the stem. Cut in half and remove the seeds. Discard the stem and seeds. **Chop** the rest of the green pepper into small pieces. Put in a small bowl.

Turn the page for more Salad Rollups

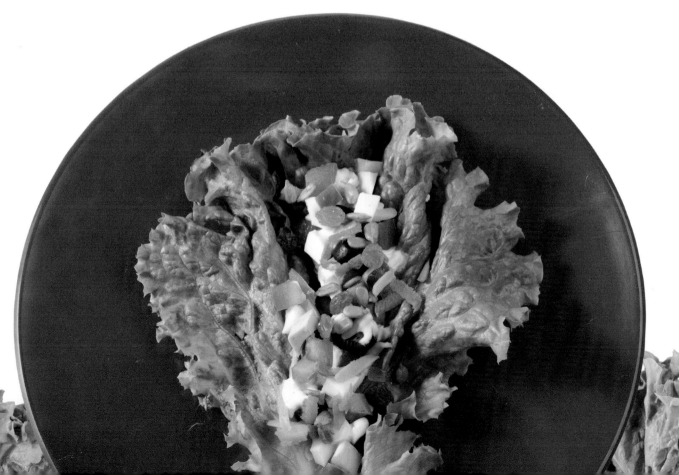

5. To cut the apple, first **cut** in half from top to bottom. Set aside one of the halves to eat or use later. Cut the other half in half again from top to bottom. Then cut out and discard the stem and seeds. **Chop** into pieces. Put in a small bowl.

6. To cut the avocado, use a knife to **cut** through the avocado the long way. (There is a large seed inside, so you can't cut all the way through.) **Pull** the two pieces apart. Set aside one half to eat or use later. **Chop** the other half in small pieces, removing the pieces from the dark peel. Put in a small bowl.

7. **Grate** carrot and place in a small bowl.

8. Wash and dry the grater. **Grate** the cheese and place in a small bowl.

9. **Place** olives, raisins or dried cranberries, and sunflower seeds in small bowls.

10. **Put** dressing ingredients together in a medium bowl. Use a fork or a whisk to **stir** until mixed.

11. Gently **pull** four large lettuce leaves from the head of lettuce. **Wash** the leaves under cool water. **Dry** with a clean dish towel.

12. **Put** a lettuce leaf on a plate. **Place** the toppings you would like in a layer over the leaf. Don't pile too high, or it will be hard to roll. You can always have seconds! **Drizzle** salad dressing on top.

13. **Fold** the bottom edge. Then **roll** leaf from one side, closing the toppings inside. Pick it up and eat. Keep a napkin handy, as it can get messy.

TRY THIS!

Try using your favorite salad dressing.

You can add anything you want to this salad. Some ideas: cottage cheese, tuna, peas, cooked beets, green onions, bean sprouts, grapes, or strawberries.

Speedy Fruit Salad

Mmmm. Nothing beats a sweet, simple fruit salad.

serves 4

preparation time: 20 minutes
cooking time: 0 minutes

ingredients:
1 cup grapes
1 apple
1 cup strawberries
1 orange
1 banana
2 tablespoons shredded coconut

equipment:
colander
measuring cup—1 cup
large bowl
knife
cutting board
large spoon
measuring spoons

1. **Wash** the grapes, apple, and strawberries in cool water. Put the grapes in the bowl.

2. **Peel** the orange. **Divide** the orange sections and put them in the bowl.

3. Use the knife and cutting board to cut fruit. **Peel** the banana and **slice** it into bite-sized rounds. **Cut** the apple into bite-sized pieces and discard the core. **Cut** the green tops off the strawberries. Then **slice** the strawberries in half. Put the banana, apple, and strawberry pieces in the bowl.

4. Gently **mix** all the fruit together with the spoon. **Sprinkle** the coconut on top of the fruit. Serve.

TRY THIS!

You can make up your own fruit salad. Use the fruit you have at home—or what's in season in your town.

Fruit is in season at different times of the year, depending on where you live. When fruit is in season, it is fresh, ripe, and ready to be eaten. Do you have a farmer's market in your town? Maybe you can buy fresh fruit from a local farmer!

serves 4 to 5

preparation time: 45 minutes
cooking time: 20 minutes

ingredients:

1 head iceberg lettuce
4 ounces (1 cup) cheddar cheese
½ cup frozen corn
1 14-ounce can black beans
4 to 5 small corn or whole
    wheat tortillas
cooking spray
⅓ pound ground beef
salsa

equipment:

knife
cutting board
measuring cups—½ cup, 1 cup
4 small bowls for toppings
grater
microwave-safe bowl
can opener
colander
pizza cutter
2 baking sheets
2 oven mitts
2 cooling racks
frying pan
wooden spoon
4 to 5 plates for
    serving

Crunchy Taco Salad

You'll make your own tortilla chips to give this salad some crunch! Serve this salad as a main dish for your family.

1. **Preheat** the oven to 400°F.

2. **Wash** the lettuce under cool water. Use the knife and cutting board to **chop** into small pieces. Place in a small bowl.

3. Use the grater to **grate** cheese. Place in a small bowl.

4. Put the corn in a microwave-safe bowl. **Warm** the frozen corn for 1 or 2 minutes in the microwave. It does not need to be hot—just not frozen. Place in a small bowl.

5. **Open** the can of black beans with a can opener. Place a colander in the sink. **Pour** the beans into the colander to drain off the liquid. Place beans in a small bowl.

6. Lay the tortillas on a cutting board. Lightly **spray** cooking spray on each side of the tortillas. Use a pizza cutter to **cut** each tortilla in 4 equal pieces.

7. Spread the tortillas on the baking sheets, and **bake** for 6 to 7 minutes. They should be a little brown. When they are done, use oven mitts to **remove** the baking sheets from the oven and set them on the cooling racks.

8. While the tortilla chips are baking, you can start cooking the ground meat. **Place** the meat in a frying pan on medium heat. Use a wooden spoon to **stir** and break up the meat. Cook until all the meat is brown. (If the meat looks pink, it is not done. Keep cooking until all the meat is brown.) Have an adult **drain** the grease out from the pan. Place the meat in a bowl.

9. **Place** 4 tortilla pieces on a plate. **Top** your taco salad with the ground beef, beans, corn, shredded lettuce, cheese, salsa, or anything else you want!

serves 4

preparation time: 30 minutes
cooking time: 20 minutes

ingredients:

1 green pepper
1 tomato
12 pepperoni slices
2 ounces (½ cup) mozzarella cheese
fresh basil (or 1 teaspoon dried basil)
6 cups water
3 cups (12 ounces) whole wheat pasta (a
   shape such as bow tie, penne, spirals,
   or shells)
½ lemon
2 tablespoons olive oil
Parmesan cheese
pepper

equipment:

serrated knife
cutting board
grater
large pot
liquid measuring cup
colander
large bowl
small bowl
small spoon
large spoon
fork

Pizza Pasta Salad

Have you ever had pizza in a bowl? This salad comes with some favorite pizza toppings. Use any shape pasta you like—bow tie, penne, spirals, or shells.

1. **Wash** the green pepper and tomato under cool water. Use the knife and cutting board to cut the vegetables. It works best to cut a tomato with a serrated knife, a knife with bumps along the sharp edge. To cut the tomato, first **cut** out the green or brown circle on the top. Discard it. Then **chop** the rest of the tomato. Set aside.

2. To cut the green pepper, first **cut** out the stem. Next, cut the green pepper in half and remove the seeds. Discard the stem and seeds. **Chop** the rest of the green pepper into small pieces. Set aside with the tomato.

3. **Cut** the pepperoni into skinny strips. Set aside with the vegetables.

4. **Grate** the cheese with a grater. Set aside with the vegetables and pepperoni.

5. If using fresh basil, **wash** it under cool water. **Pull** the leaves off the stem. **Tear** the leaves into small pieces or **chop** with a knife on the cutting board. Measure 2 tablespoons and set aside.

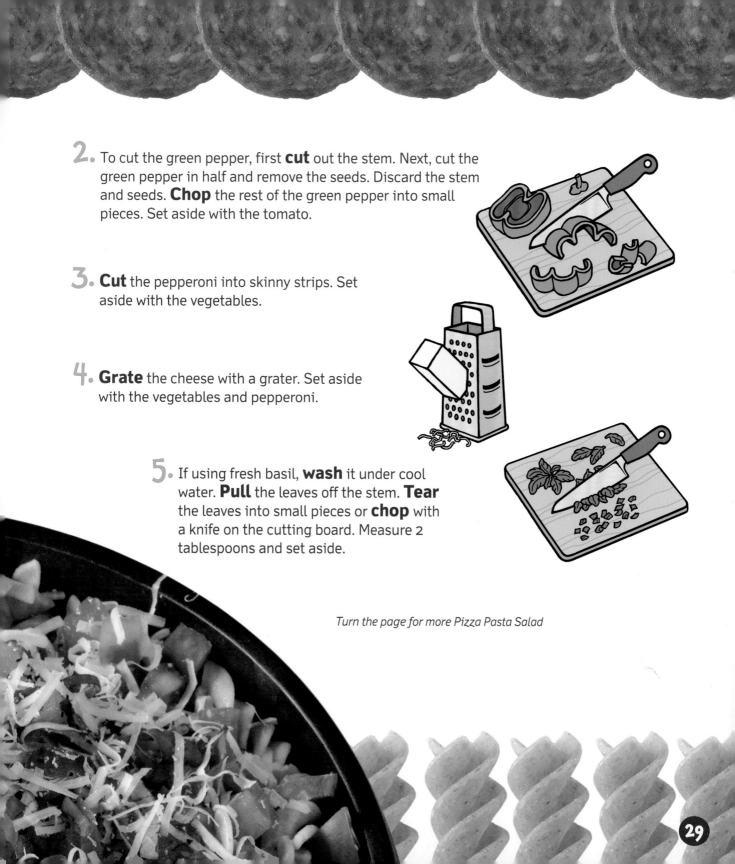

Turn the page for more Pizza Pasta Salad

6. In a large pot, bring 6 cups water to a boil. **Add** the pasta. Follow the directions on the pasta package for the cooking time.

7. When the pasta is done cooking, have an adult **drain** the pasta into a colander. Run cold water over the pasta. **Pour** the pasta into a large bowl.

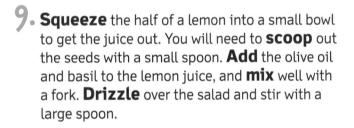

8. **Add** green pepper, tomato, pepperoni, and mozzarella cheese. **Stir** until well mixed.

9. **Squeeze** the half of a lemon into a small bowl to get the juice out. You will need to **scoop** out the seeds with a small spoon. **Add** the olive oil and basil to the lemon juice, and **mix** well with a fork. **Drizzle** over the salad and stir with a large spoon.

10. **Sprinkle** Parmesan cheese and pepper on top. Serve.

TRY THIS!
You can add any of your other favorite pizza toppings, such as chopped olives or spinach.

SPECIAL INGREDIENTS

avocado: a large, egg-shaped fruit with dark green bumpy or smooth skin, bright green flesh, and a large pit. Avocados can be found in the produce section of grocery stores.

basil: the leaves of a basil plant. Fresh basil can be found with other fresh herbs in the produce section of grocery stores. Dried basil is located in the dried spice and herb section.

bok choy: a type of cabbage, also called Chinese cabbage. You can find bok choy in the produce section of many grocery stores.

broth or stock: the liquid part of a soup is called broth or stock. Look for it in the soup section of a grocery store. It comes in cans, cartons, and small jars. (Read the directions for use.)

chili powder: a blend of dried, ground spices, often used to flavor chili. Look for it in the dried spice and herb section of your grocery store.

creamed corn: partially pureed corn mixed with several other ingredients. It is sold in cans and can be found in the vegetable aisle of grocery stores.

cumin: the dried fruit of a plant in the parsley family used to flavor many Middle Eastern and Asian dishes. Look for ground cumin in the dried spice and herb section of your grocery store.

egg roll skins: thin squares of dough. You can find egg roll skins in many large grocery stores. Look in the produce section or the refrigerated section. You can also find egg roll skins at Asian grocery stores.

red potato: a type of potato with thin, red skin. It can be found in the produce section of grocery stores.

salsa: a sauce that may contain tomatoes, hot peppers, garlic, and herbs. It is often used to flavor Mexican dishes and can be found near the chips in the snack food aisle of the grocery store.

shredded coconut: the dried, sweetened flesh of the coconut. It can be found in the baking aisle of most grocery stores.

soy sauce: a salty sauce often used in Chinese and Japanese dishes. Look for it in the ethnic foods section of most grocery stores.

wonton wrappers: thin squares of dough that are smaller than egg roll skin. You can find wonton wrappers in many large grocery stores. Look in the produce section or the refrigerated section. You can also find wonton wrappers at Asian grocery stores.

FURTHER READING AND WEBSITES

ChooseMyPlate.gov
http://www.choosemyplate.gov
/children-over-five.html
Download coloring pages, play an
interactive computer game, and get
lots of nutrition information at this U.S.
Department of Agriculture website.

**Cleary, Brian P. Food Is CATegorical
series. Minneapolis: Millbrook Press, 2011.**
This seven-book illustrated series offers
a fun introduction to the food groups and
other important health information.

Farmers Markets Search
http://apps.ams.usda.gov/FarmersMarkets/
Visit this site to find a farmer's market near
you!

Katzen, Mollie. *Salad People and More Real
Recipes: A New Cookbook for Preschoolers
& Up.* Berkeley, CA: Tricycle Press, 2005.
This cookbook offers twenty vegetarian
recipes that kids can make with some help
from adults.

Recipes
http://www.sproutonline.com
/crafts-and-recipes/recipes
Find more fun and easy recipes for kids at
this site.

INDEX